T0084980

Let's Celebrate!

A Can-You-Find-It Book

by Sarah L. Schuette

PEBBLE
a capstone imprint

Seasons

Can you find
these things?

guitar

cat

snail

taco

 tractor

 cherries

 skateboard

 pie

 zebra

 wagon

Fiesta!

Can you find
these things?

 spider

 pineapple

 avocado

 nose

 key

 llama

 pig

 hanger

 sun

 rose

Happy Birthday

Can you find these things?

goldfish

poodle

tennis ball

helicopter

 car

 rainbow

 cell phone

 frog

 seahorse

 piñata

Fireworks

Can you find
these things?

milk jug   flute   penguin   hockey skate

 astronaut

 shovel

 skunk

 crown

 ax

 orca

Gift Card

Can you find
these things?

caterpillar

Earth

tent

palm
tree

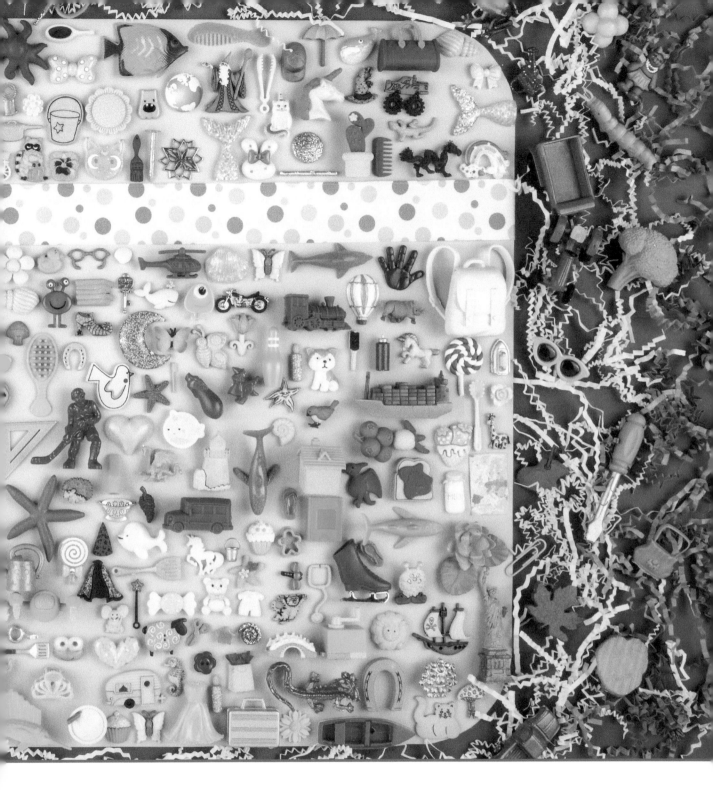

 cup

 owl

 surfboard

 gift bag

paperclip

 eggplant

Love

Can you find these things?

mitten

bird

candle

roller skate

fire
truck

crab

chicken

lips

watermelon

ballet
shoes

Holiday Break

Can you find these things?

 tape

 pickle

 moon

 trumpet

 airplane

 hot dog

 cactus

 strawberry

 pear

 corncob

Día de los Muertos

Can you find these things?

umbrella

grapes

bicycle

shark

 flamingo

 hot air balloon

 starfish

 ice-cream cone

 mushroom

 pumpkin

Trick or Treat?

Can you find these things?

 snowman

 basketball

 rocking horse

 grill

Santa's hat   ping-pong paddle   firefighter   cowboy hat   clamshell   cupcake

Trim the Tree

Can you find
these things?

unicorn

heart

pizza

horseshoe

 pliers

 ghost

 flashlight

 spoon

 snowflake

 carrot

light bulb

camera

cake

clover

drum   stapler   apple   cookies   rake   rat

Earth Day

Can you find
these things?

wrench

tissue
box

pants

toaster

heart

book

candy
cane

cow

star

blender

Lucky Day!

Can you find
these things?

mermaid

elephant

anchor

button

puppy

milkshake

ladybug

spatula

sailboat

moose

spray
bottle

trophy

bird

knife

Turn the page for the answer key!

 red pepper

 microphone

 caterpillar

 toilet paper

 sandwich

 broccoli

Psst! Did you know that Pebs the Pebble was hiding
in EVERY PUZZLE in this book?

It's true! Go back and look!

Hi.

Look for all the other books in this series:

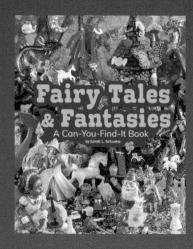
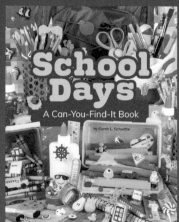
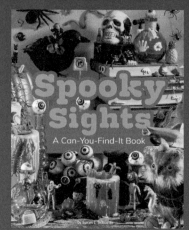

The author dedicates this book to her nieces, Ava and Faith Hahn.

Pebble Sprout is published by Pebble, an imprint of Capstone.
1710 Roe Crest Drive, North Mankato, Minnesota 56003
www.capstonepub.com

Library of Congress Cataloging-in-Publication Data is available on the Library of Congress website.
Names: Schuette, Sarah L., 1976- author.
Title: Let's celebrate! : a can-you-find-it book / by Sarah L. Schuette.
Description: North Mankato : Pebble, 2020. | Series: Can you find it? | Audience: Ages 4-8 (provided by Pebble) | Description based on print version record and CIP data provided by publisher; resource not viewed.
Identifiers: LCCN 2019057497 (print) | LCCN 2019057498 (ebook)
ISBN 9781977122599 (library binding) | ISBN 9781977126252 (paperback)
ISBN 9781977123114 (eBook PDF)
Subjects: LCSH: Schools—Juvenile literature. | Picture puzzles—Juvenile literature.
Classification: LCC LB1556 (ebook) | LCC LB1556 .S38 2020 (print) | DDC 793.73—dc23 LC record available at https://lccn.loc.gov/2019057497

Image Credits
All photos by Capstone Studio: Karon Dubke

Editorial Credits
Shelly Lyons, editor; Heidi Thompson, designer; Marcy Morin, set stylist; Morgan Walters, media researcher; Kathy McColley, production specialist